GET CLEAR

Craft and Deliver Impactful Presentations Worth Hearing

❧ Sandra Van de Cauter ❧

ISBN: 978-1-48359-361-6 (print)
ISBN: 978-1-48359-362-3 (ebook)

GET CLEAR: FOREWORD

I am a good presenter. It's part of what I do: stand in front of a crowd and convince them to change their behavior, start down a new path, and even (gasp!) give me money for it. I'm comfortable on stage and enjoy standing in the light.

It wasn't always that way. I've overcome my share of stage fright episodes, mid-talk flubs and blanks. There were presentations that didn't connect, talks after which I thought 'why were so many people not paying attention?' True, it didn't happen a lot. But just once could make me question the entire structure and content of a previously successful presentation.

Then I met Sandra in a local business network. I mentioned that I was trying to get a large company in town to give me a speaking engagement, and she shared her approach to successful corporate speaking. Her philosophy was different, and it made perfect sense. I tried it at my next meeting with them and it worked!

As time went on, Sandra and I continued to talk about speaking – and about all the preparation that (should) go into a presentation. I began implementing her advice, using the tips and questions that you'll find in this book. Now they are part of my regular routine. I have learned to 'get clear' – about my audience, my goals, and most importantly, my motivation. What a difference! I spend less time writing scripts and decks and more time enjoying a conversation with my audience.

Presenting effectively is one of the most important and most under-valued business skills. In corporate life, ineffective presentations waste time and can lead to poor decision-making. Make a few bad business decisions in a row and you can bring down a business. Make a few good ones and you can transform it for the better. If you speak for a living, the stakes are even higher; a few bad presentations can kill your business!

Effective presenting can be learned; most of us must work at it. The question is, who will teach us? The explosion of TED and TED-like programs creates an expectation that everyone can 'talk like TED.' But how? Personal coaches are expensive. The company programs and workshops I've attended were tactical and didn't make a lasting change. Too many of the books I've seen are too long and compli-cated. 'Get Clear' is different.

Sandra Van de Cauter knows all about creating and delivering effec-tive presentations. She's a Distinguished Toastmaster - the highest level that speakers can attain from Toastmasters International. She's also a top corporate communications coach. Sandra has taught entrepreneurs, middle managers and senior corporate executives to deliver focused messages that inform, persuade, and encourage clear thinking and effective decisions.

Sandra's advice is straightforward. Her process is simple. It forces you to think, not only about your content, but about your role in the communication, your audience's role, and the journey you will take together over the course of your presentation.

I know, because she helped me. Working with Sandra, I moved from a confident and effective speaker to a completely new level. There were no 'mystical secrets,' no magic shortcuts. The magic came from putting the time, thought, and effort into the right areas. Like so many transformative programs, you start by thinking. The difference was in the questions she asked. You must examine far more than your content to really connect with your audience, and give them what they need. You must also examine yourself.

If you're in a business environment, communication, persuasion, and decisions are the fabric of your daily life. Do them well and you will be successful. Understand what's behind them, 'get clear' on your motivations, your audience's needs, and the essential facts, and you will succeed. Time and again, Sandra's process has helped me to convince, to educate, to persuade and to do business. Invest your time and energy, and it will help you too.

With "Get Clear," Sandra Van de Cauter makes a valuable contribution to the growing library of communication and presentation books. Speakers, and their audiences, owe her their thanks.

Dr. Marne Platt is a former corporate executive, business consultant and founder of Fundamental Capabilities. She is also the author of Living Singlish: Your Life, Your Way, a book filled with practical tips for young women building independent lives and learning to stand on their own two feet.

They have more experience than me.

I get nervous speaking to a large audience.

I do not like questions asked after my presentation.

They will make fun of my accent.

I will draw a blank and forget my text.

When you can relate to one of these concerns, you will benefit from this book..

I do not like presenting other people's slides.

I do not have time to prepare or rehearse.

I do not like presenting on stage.

I do not like presenting to senior management.

I do not have enough expertise.

INTRODUCTION

The world of communication runs like a common thread throughout my career since 1998. From teaching communication courses, conflict handling and career coaching for employees to focusing on presentations, moderation and public speaking.

Communication is such an important aspect in every part of the business. Yet not enough attention is given to this crucial skill. I have been coaching leaders from all levels with their business presentations in or outside the company. What struck me the most were the reasons why the leaders experienced stress. Between the leadership levels the similarities for stress was strikingly similar. Their education, their experiences or even the fact that they had already presented a hundred times didn't matter. There were moments when a certain presentation was too much stress to handle alone.

My approach focused on three main aspects: prepare, rehearse and deliver. It was a very simple method yet effective. Paying attention to the objective and the content of the presentation, the aspects of the environment where the presentation would take place, as well as the specific needs of the audience.

Throughout the years I noticed that my approach was mostly successful but sometimes the results were so different than intended. It bothered me and made me wonder what the reason could be for this lack of success.

A few years ago, while coaching a senior executive, a big AHA! moment turned my coaching approach upside down. This book is built upon the findings of this AHA! moment and provides the newly created approach: GET CLEAR. This approach has been experienced by dozens of leaders of all levels presenting in or outside the company. It has proven to be successful every time.

I am convinced that reading this book will help you understand the core reason for success or failure while presenting and will help you get clear.

The business needs people to speak up. Let's remove whatever stress is holding you from presenting and let's focus on what matters.

We need to hear you speak because your message matters.

THE STORY

The AHA Moment

A few years ago Jennifer, a senior executive, contacted me. She had been invited to speak at a large event about women and leadership. Although Jennifer had given many presentations, this one was causing significant stress. Within the company, Jennifer was known as a confident speaker and an inspirational leader. Her colleagues were convinced that she would master this challenge without any problems. They all admired her speaking skills. But Jennifer realized that this time she needed support. She sensed that there is a difference between speaking with confidence about a job-related topic within the company and speaking with confidence about a business related topic outside of the company.

Jennifer and I began our journey. We worked together over the course of a few weeks following a simple 3 step approach of prepare, rehearse and deliver. Gathering all the information we could about location, audience, and working the key messages went smoothly until we noticed difficulty with crafting the content. And then one night, I awoke at 3 am, thinking:

> *"Why doesn't it work? What is missing? We took into account all the different elements. We revised the text and got clear on the key messages. We have been working together for a few weeks and suddenly it feels like we are 10 steps back. What is happening? What is holding us back and making us doubt? Jennifer and I will talk about this first thing in our next coaching session."*

The next day, before editing the content I proposed to review all the details of the event.

'Let's take it from the beginning, Jennifer. Let's recap the whole setting of the event, and go into each detail again, let's find the answer to the who, what, where, when, how and why.'

It became clear that these previously discussed details about the event had a higher significance and impact then we had assumed.

Details like:

- There would be a delegation from the company including Jennifer's manager attending.

- There would be significant global visibility with radio interviews and live broadcasting.

- It would attract a global audience and a number of experienced top women speakers.

- Jennifer had never spoken during such an important event outside the company.

- Her performance could have a vast impact on her career, positive or negative.

These details now caught my attention and especially the last reflection was alerting us. Accepting the invitation to speak unconsciously conjured up an expectation that speaking could 'make or break' Jennifer's career.

'Make is fine, but break? Hmm…wait a second.'

After a moment, I asked Jennifer:

'Why speak?' 'Under these circumstances, with a daily heavy workload, with no prior experience, all the additional stress from the presence of top speakers, a company delegation, live- broadcasting and radio, significant global visibility, and a performance that could make or break your career, why did you agree to speak? Honestly, with the odds against you, why would anyone agree to go through with this?' This was a paramount 'aha' moment for both of us.

Until this moment my coaching had been focused around the objective of the presentation. Such as to inform employees, to ask for approval, to negotiate contracts, to motivate or engage a team, and to highlight achievements are some examples.

And although I knew that everyone wants 'something' for themselves from a presentation until that moment I had never thought about the weight of this reason. Accepting a speaking invitation installs a chain reaction impacting the presenter and collides with the preparation of the presentation.

Basically, the underlying question we unraveled was 'what's in it for Jennifer?

It's this 'something' that needs the presenter's full attention prior to writing down the first word of the presentation. I realized in that moment that unless we paid attention Jennifer and I would be running in circles and running out of time.

MEET YOUR PERSONAL MOTIVATION

What is this 'something'?

It's your personal motivation to accept to speak. It's what drove you to say yes, what you were thinking you could get from presenting. It's different from the presentations objective. A new person on a team could have been asked to give a presentation about themselves to the team. The presentations objective would then be a personal introduction. But the personal motivation could be something like wanting to impress the new team, establishing you are the right hire and showcase your expertise.

Most of the time we are not fully aware of our personal motivation. This was the same for Jennifer. Naming exactly what she wanted wasn't so straightforward. As we considered it more closely we discovered many different elements like daring to try something new,

7

making a dream come true, making a good impression, having the experience of being a key note speaker and much more. A personal motivation is always a collection of expectations and can be complex. It was complex AND very alive. A personal motivation is real.

The moment you agree to speak your personal motivation only grows stronger, longing to manifest your expectations. It interferes, interrupts and intrudes. It influences every detail of your presentation when you prepare, rehearse and deliver. It affects your word choice; slide content, your clothing choice, your stage presence, and your voice. It affects the way you perceive and interpret your audience's behavior.

It functions like a little voice telling you what to do, whom to impress, whom to pay attention to. This little voice talks on and on. It can drive speakers crazy. No wonder that public speaking is referred to as the number one fear.

Working with, Jennifer, I suddenly understood why some of the people I had coached previously had been successful while others hadn't. Whose personal motivations might have interfered?

The experience with Jennifer connected all the dots and helped me understand that gaining clarity about what drives you, what your personal motivation really is, is critical.

We found ourselves changing or editing the content constantly before we realized Jennifer's motivation was interfering. When we knew what was happening, we consciously refocused on what mattered. We then were able to gain clarity about the real key messages of the presentation and remove everything that wasn't relevant.

With renewed focus and excitement still running high, we continued. We were both looking forward to her big moment. We imagined her speaking successfully. Things were going great.

And then it all changed *again*.

A few weeks before the event we ran into obstacles. Some rehearsals were interrupted or were postponed, and again slide and speech content changes. Jennifer wasn't 100% sure about the key messages. And she had started to doubt herself. Neither of us knew what was happening but it felt like we were back to square one again. 'What's going on?' I thought. 'We were doing so well!'

By now we knew to pause and take the time to address what was happening. During our conversation Jennifer shared *all* her worst-case scenarios. We spent the session giving voice to each worrisome or troubling thought that felt as if it was happening now. These worst-case scenarios felt real. They were a serious concern driving Jennifer to try to escape from feeling her emotions. Some of her escaping techniques were procrastination, constantly changing the presentations content and being reluctant to rehearse. These reactions were setting Jennifer unwittingly up for failure. She lost her excitement, her enthusiasm and became a victim of her doom and gloom downward spiral. This awareness completed the AHA! moment. This is the moment I realized that your personal motivation could turn against you and sabotage.

Yes, the personal motivation, that 'drive' that gets you excited to speak, can also drive you nuts. Once you realize that what you wish for might not happen, the fear of failure will play a game with you. What was discovered and discussed during this coaching session were two elements to the downward spiral: the things you can influence and things that you can't.

We made two lists. Our first list focused on what we could influence. We examined each scenario and looked for the elements, which we could influence. We realized that having assumptions was causing the stress. Assumptions about everything like the audience, event logistics or expectations. We addressed these assumptions by creating an action list with points that required further clarification from the event organizers.

The second list included the assumptions or expectations that you cannot influence or control like the audience's behavior during your presentation. When you believe what you assume is true your brain simply looks for the proof of your assumptions and will find it. This list required extensive coaching. The following technique helped define the underlying core belief driving the assumptions.

For example: We used one of the most stressful assumptions. When mirroring back the assumption to Jennifer I asked what it would mean to her when this assumption would manifest? It went like this 'when (assumption) happens that means that…'

We repeated this question to each response she gave until we arrived at the underlying core belief. We knew it was the core belief because we could not find a response beyond it. This core belief was the driver and carried Jennifer's biggest bottom line fear; 'this presentation could break my career". As we worked through all assumptions, it turned out that all of them were driven by this core fear. There is always a level of drama attached to an assumption. Exposing the drama attached to the assumption began to dissolve the impact of the core belief.

The result of getting clear turned the saboteur back to an ally. Our focus returned to creating an impactful presentation worth hearing. The excitement filled the room leaving us with a sigh of relief. This cycle of ally-saboteur-ally is a part of getting clear. Expect this to be a part of your process to get clear.

When the big day came, Jennifer was ready. Because she had experience with keeping her focus on the presentation, she was emotionally freed up to keep her calm during unplanned interviews prior to her talk. When she went on stage she tackled an unforeseen protocol challenge and gave a polished, professional and highly inspiring performance. She kept her personal motivation on her side by remaining focused on the content of her presentation; the reward was an engaged audience listening in awe.

Jennifer was rated as a top speaker of the event, vastly exceeding her own expectations. Since then we have worked together on a few more presentations and every time Jennifer was quick to spot who was really driving her presentation, the ally or the saboteur.

She has successfully given other presentations outside of the company boosting her career even further. And she loves every bit of it. While keeping her focus on what matters for the audience she is able to have her personal motivation come true: a Win-Win situation.

Take Responsibility for Your Performance

Being a successful presenter means taking full responsibility for your performance. Many people blame their poor performance on lack of preparation time. They blame it on the fact that they are presenting someone else's slides or they are stepping in at the last minute. Maybe so, but who cares?

Your audience doesn't care whether or not you had time to prepare, or whether you are jumping in for someone else. They simply do not care. It is not their task to care.

They do care if they need to listen to an unprepared speaker who is wasting their time. The audience remembers the speaker's performance. So, excusing yourself in the beginning of a presentation doesn't really help. On the contrary, it irritates the audience.

Backing out of a presentation isn't the solution either. Learn to use the time you have wisely and learn to keep your personal motivation on your side even with last minute notification. The approach described in this book will help you use your time wisely keeping you focused on what matters. You need to take full responsibility for yourself and your performance. Everyone can deliver a clear message worth hearing.

Jennifer's story shows us that a personal motivation can be an excellent driver. It can push you to stretch beyond your comfort zone. It also shows us that the personal motivation can sabotage you. Jennifer's story could be yours. Whether you are a senior executive or newly employed, you can experience significant stress when presenting. To perform at your best, you need to keep your focus on what really matters and what you can influence as presenter.

In the next chapter we will walk through the different stages of 'Get Clear'.

Discover what you can and cannot influence. Every stage has a specific focus, describing what a presenter needs to get clear about to craft and deliver a presentation worth hearing.

We are ready for your message. Are you ready to deliver it?

GET CLEAR

Introducing The 4 Stages

People experience a good presentation when they get something from it.

It's that simple.

We will use Jennifer's presentation to explain how we defined the right content for her audience. The reference guide has all the questions to use for preparing your own presentation.

There are 4 stages for crafting and delivering a presentation worth hearing;

| FOCUS | PREPARE | REHEARSE | DELIVER |

Moving through the stages you focus on what matters, invest your time wisely and gain clarity to create the key messages resulting in a Win-Win situation for you and your audience.

Stage 1 Focus

FOCUS	PREPARE	REHEARSE	DELIVER

Finding Your Personal Motivation: What's In It For You?

When Jennifer was vaguely aware of her personal motivation it unconsciously had a full grip on her behavior. It made Jennifer excited at first, then anxious and then excited again. It was providing the energy to start preparing and rehearsing then suddenly driving her into procrastination and sabotage every element of the presentation.

Knowing your personal motivation is crucial to your success. Once you name it, you will notice how and when it acts as an ally or your saboteur. We can't know what we don't know.

Avoiding finding your personal motivation doesn't make the personal motivation disappear.

On the contrary your personal motivation is there and is very active but you will be unaware of its influence. It will be reflected in the content, in your slides, in your voice, in your body language and in your stage presence.

Your personal motivation is built up from your expectations. When you accept to speak you do it because you see the opportunities for you. The personal motivation is linked to two scenarios, a best-case and a worst-case. It is important to define in detail both scenarios as both contain elements you can or you cannot influence.

Defining both scenarios in detail in the same session is the key to stopping the ally saboteur roller coaster. The ally will focus on the elements you can influence while the saboteur focuses on the elements that you cannot influence. Both the ally and saboteur will look for proof to support the beliefs you hold. In order to deliver impactful presentations worth hearing focus on what you can influence while being willing to let go of what you cannot influence. This will release the saboteur and help you gain time.

Had I known what I know now I would have asked Jenifer the following sets of questions sequentially. However we followed this new approach with her next presentations. For the sake of making the process clear to you I will address the questions as described in the reference guide.

It would have saved us so much time and suffering if I had asked Jennifer a few questions to get clear about her personal motivation. At first I wanted to know what her personal benefits could be. It certainly could influence her career when she performed well. A good performance could also make her a highly requested speaker overnight. Speaking at this event was definitely a big opportunity to do something different, something new, and something exciting.

Jennifer always liked to further develop herself and this invitation looked like a great opportunity to break out of her comfort zone.

To experience these successes what should take place during or after her presentation? I wanted to know how she would 'know' when she was successful. What will she pay attention to which would prove her successes. While presenting, a speaker seeks signs of proof for success like noticing that the audience is engaged or the technology works without glitches. For Jennifer success was these things and she imagined receiving new speaking opportunities when connecting with her audience after the presentation.

Now we knew the best-case scenario. After our AHA! moment we investigated the other side of the coin. What would be the worst-case scenario that she could experience that day?

The worst that could happen for Jennifer was drawing a blank while speaking and providing a bad delivery, experiencing a non-engaged audience, technology failure, and making a very bad impression disappointing the company and jeopardizing her career opportunities.

Answering the best and worst-case questions allowed the unconscious expectations and fears to surface. They are always present and playing tricks on you. They can make you exaggerate, complicate your message or confuse the audience as you look to impress them. You become more interested in overselling yourself or the message than in providing relevant impactful content. When the personal motivation was playing a trick on Jennifer, she started to embellish her presentation causing the content to drift from clarity into confusion.

The only way out is to keep your focus on what matters for the audience. Jennifer could gain benefit from the presentation as long as the content of the presentation fully mattered to the audience.

An in-depth description of Jennifer's personal motivation functioned as a reference guide to provide insight of the sabotaging activities. We kept that document at hand. It was our compass to navigate through the next 3 stages. The ally-saboteur roller coaster is unpredictable; the only way out is getting clear in the moment. When Jennifer started to doubt, edit content or procrastinate we knew what was happening. Exposing the activity and talking about it, helped to regain focus on what was relevant and on what she could influence.

Stage 2 Prepare

FOCUS	**PREPARE**	REHEARSE	DELIVER

The power of a presentation lies in telling exactly what is necessary to the people who need to hear it in the format that makes sense.

When Jennifer approached me she had already written content and created slides. She hadn't begun at the beginning but instead at mid point. Creating a PowerPoint presentation is often considered sufficient preparation. That's not true; slides are only one-way to present, and are not always necessary. Take a conscious, well thought-out decision about whether you need them. Avoid doing it out of habit. Although PowerPoint presentations are often standard in business, creating them will be the *last* activity of this stage.

The Prepare stage paves the road to create clear and impactful presentations. Jumping this stage makes rehearsing and delivering difficult, as your content might be confusing.

What is this stage all about? It's getting as much information as possible about the event, logistics, your audience and their expectations. The more you know the better you will be prepared by reducing the chances for surprises. This serves two purposes: on one hand it will help lower your stress levels and on the other hand it will set you up for writing the relevant content for your audience. Gathering information helps you win time. Instead of rushing something you can edit fifty times, gather information and focus on what matters.

We knew that Jennifer's event was outside the company. Getting a full picture helped us understand the real challenges. It was a global audience with potential interruptions of people entering and leaving at any time. It was being recorded, and later we found out it was also live TV with Radio broadcasting. She would be speaking on stage using a microphone. She was asked to speak from her experience as a senior woman executive. She opted to use slides and had a fix deadline to send the slide deck. That's what we knew.

For most people this would be enough information to start writing the presentation. But it isn't. You first need to have all the details clear to avoid surprises. During the coaching session after the AHA! moment we discovered we did not know enough details to deal with the levels of stress she was experiencing and to finalize the content.

We delved into logistics. We looked online to find images of previous events at the same location. This gave us a better idea of the floor plan, seating arrangements, stage and supporting technology. I had questions about the microphone, as it is such an important piece of technology that stresses many speakers. I insisted on Jennifer asking for a headset instead of a clip-on microphone. A headset offers you the possibility to turn your head freely without interfering with the sound quality and also provides more choices for clothing options.

On that note I asked Jennifer if there was a dress code? Was there a protocol to pay attention to?

Would Jennifer be introduced? By whom and who provides the introduction text? Writing your own introduction text is highly recommended or at least find out what was written for you prior to preparing your content.

As Jennifer was using slides, I asked what type of slide changer was being used. Could she bring her own? Using an unfamiliar slide changer can be nerve-wracking for a presenter.

Jennifer had to send in her presentation prior but in what format? What software version are the organizers using? I asked if she could use animation in the presentation or did it need to be without? How big is the screen? How high is the screen? Can she use the stage or is she bound to a lectern or a designated place on stage? We prepared for everything that we could influence. Taking charge reduces stress and raises self-confidence, plus it provides a plan B in case of surprises.

Until now we hadn't even addressed the content of the presentation. We addressed the details of the event. Most presenters lack interest in these details, they assume instead. A maybe or possibly is not clear. Get clear. Avoid assuming; it's the number one trap for most presenters. It creates unpleasant surprises.

Once the event details had been clarified with Jennifer we were able to review the existing content. While editing the text we based our approach on two quotations.

'Perfection is not when there is no more to add but when there is no more to take away'

–Antoine de Saint-Exupéry

'Do not say a little in many words but a great deal in a few'

–Pythagoras

The personal motivation can trick you in editing the content only to serve you while being totally irrelevant for the audience. We spent quite some time reviewing and editing. To find out which content to keep, I repeated continuously two words, 'who cares!' I played the devil's advocate while also challenging the answer by questioning 'so what?'

Stripping the content from all space fillers and deviations, and scrutinizing slides and images on relevance and impact culminated in a crisp and powerful content with a slide deck that supported every element of the presentation adapted to the audience.

Most presenters stop here until the day they deliver. What about rehearsing?

Stage 3 Rehearse

FOCUS	PREPARE	**REHEARSE**	DELIVER

Everybody rehearses; most of us rehearse when
we deliver.

Speaking out loud for the first time is called rehearsing. If your first spoken words out loud happen in front of your audience you are rehearsing while delivering. I cannot count the number of surprised faces I see when I explain this.

A good presenter is often described as a 'natural' speaker. I do not believe in the natural speaker concept. Some people have fewer issues presenting, that's true. But everyone needs to rehearse to perform well.

In reality most people skip rehearsing and step directly into delivering. Reading the content of your slides a couple of times is not the same as rehearsing and will not transform you into an inspirational speaker either.

The main excuse put forward in the business to skip rehearsing is 'lack of time'. Maybe so, but who cares? Not your audience. Your credibility is on the line. Would you prefer to be remembered as someone who spoke but didn't say much? Or would you prefer to be remembered as someone who was clear and made sense?

Invest the time you have wisely. When your time is limited find your key message by focusing on what really matters, use the stages to create clear content. This facilitates the rehearsing.

Rehearsing is all about reducing stress to the absolute possible minimum. When you rehearse you take away the stress of the 'first time'. Who wouldn't want to do that?

How did Jennifer rehearse? Certainly not by reading her slides in silence or notes cards.

Rehearsals happened out loud. She took time in between meetings, in the car, at home and of course during our planned rehearsals. We focused on the content, or the PPT presentation or had stage rehearsals.

As Jennifer would speak on a stage, it was beneficial for her to experience what it is like to be called on stage. Walking on stage is challenging. How fast do you walk? How big are your steps? Do you look in front of you or do you look at the audience? How will you hold your hands? Being watched from a large audience with high expectations can make a speaker's heart race.

Numerous rehearsals of walking silently on stage highlighted the moments Jennifer became nervous and the thoughts behind her nerves. Every time Jennifer would experience nervousness, we would pause, and check in on her thoughts. We realized that the nervousness was the personal motivation sabotaging Jennifer.

Every time Jennifer's thoughts would drift, we would drive the attention back to the purpose of the presentation and content. Bringing your focus back to the content has an immediate effect of calming you down and gaining clarity with confidence. Of course this implies that your content is fully relevant to you audience.

Rehearsing out loud helped Jennifer to create clean transitions between the slides, helped to choose the appropriate words to emphasize and to realize which words caused difficulties in pronunciation. This is why you need to rehearse out loud.

I challenged Jennifer to rehearse in front of the mirror at least one time. The hardest feedback often comes from the presenters themselves. It helped Jennifer to find out how much self-criticism was active and also for her to realize she was pretty good.

One day, Jennifer had a hard time finding her speaking voice. Nerves were getting a hold of her and she was a flat monotone. I introduced a game to loosen her up. I asked Jennifer to present the first 10 lines, as if it was the funniest thing she had ever said; play, pretend, be silly. Although it was difficult at first it soon helped her to loosen up and it got us both laughing.

After that, Jennifer repeated these same lines as if they were the most serious matter on Earth. She played it well and we got some laughs out of that too. She warmed and loosened up. I then asked her to take a deep breath, focus on the content, pause, look up and begin. Out came a voice perfectly in sync with the meaning of the message.

The saboteur can make you sound extremely serious. It can drive you into stiff delivery and defensive body language. Exaggeration cracks the grip the saboteur has on the presenter. We played until the grip was broken.

If you want to take anything serious then it is rehearsing. Jennifer took rehearsals seriously.

Stage 4 Deliver

FOCUS	PREPARE	REHEARSE	**DELIVER**

Your delivery starts from the moment you enter
the location until you leave.

As a speaker you will be scrutinized from the moment you are seen
until the moment you are out of sight. Your behavior will be evaluated by the audience's expectation of you being the expert during the
entire event. How the speaker manages the elements of surprise adds
to the credibility of the speaker. Because you have been rehearsing
you are prepared to handle challenges of last minute changes, and
elements of surprise.

From our last dress rehearsal I gave Jennifer a few tips to alleviate
her stress and keep her personal motivation as an ally throughout
the whole delivery. Knowing that she would be on her own in a new
location surrounded by an unfamiliar environment with high expectations we anticipated this would be an arena for the worst or best-case scenario to manifest. The saboteur is behind the scenes waiting
for an opportunity to seize the moment and run the show.

I gave Jennifer a tip to warm up her voice before presenting. When
presenters are tense they have the tendency to mumble. Warm up
your voice by reciting tongue twisters. They are fun exercises and not

only beneficial for pronunciation but keeps you in a playful mood which pushes the saboteur away. The saboteur controls situations and demands seriousness. Fun and play is the antidote to seriousness.

Jennifer's stress had transformed into excitement and anticipating being the best she could be. I knew she was ready and I asked her to focus on having fun and enjoying the experience.

Because Jennifer had rehearsed well and truly believed in her message, she had put all the odds on her side. Jennifer rehearsed a graceful entry on stage and had a strong opening for her presentation. During presenting she was able to use her note cards appropriately while also using the lectern. She used pauses to perfection and emphasized her key messages to engage the audience. Even with a racing heart, Jennifer, was having fun. She could do this, as she knew her presentation inside out.

Jennifer is an inspirational speaker; some people would refer to her as a 'natural'. Never underestimate the amount of work she put into becoming a natural. Jennifer is a professional presenter who understands that delivering impactful presentations worth hearing requires getting and staying clear.

ALLY OR SABOTEUR

How active is your personal motivation?

While working with Jennifer I noticed that her personal motivation sabotaged her on a regular basis. It happened during the preparation and rehearsal and she noticed it even showed up during her delivery.

How can you recognize that your personal motivation is on your side or is sabotaging you?

A quick and accurate indicator is noticing how you feel. When you feel relaxed, excited or content, your personal motivation is functioning as your ally. When you feel nervous, irritated, and anxious, your personal motivation will switch into sabotaging activities.

Although there is a clear distinction between both, realizing in the moment which part is active isn't always that easy. Especially as your personal motivation has a tendency to jump from being your ally one moment into being the saboteur the next moment. As a presenter you need to pay attention to what is steering you the whole time.

Here are signs that can help you identify which part is activated.

Signs that your personal motivation functions as your Ally

- You want to prepare a presentation tailored to your audience

- You don't assume, you find facts

- You know what you can influence

- You invest time in rehearsing

- You keep your focus on what is relevant

You will notice that you want to be active, be eager to invest time wisely and be interested in your audience. These are all signs that your personal motivation is your Ally.

Signs that your personal motivation functions as your Saboteur

- You invest as little time as possible in preparation

- You want to impress with information that high-lights your achievements

– You don't consider rehearsing important
and procrastinate

– You start your presentation with an excuse (lack of
time, substitute, not your slides)

– You skim the audience and interpret their behavior

Looking for excuses NOT to do something is your strong indicator that you are sabotaging yourself. In the worst-case scenario, people who do not want to present can even fall sick, arrive late, get stuck in traffic or even lose their voice temporarily.

What can you do when the personal motivation is sabotaging you?

During the preparation stage find a quiet space, take the questions of the reference guide and answer them. They might not all be relevant for your presentation but they will give you a quick indication of how much information you have and what you still need to gather.

When you notice you don't want to answer the questions, ask yourself if you are fine to risk unpleasant surprises. When you jump into creating slides, ask yourself for every slide you create, 'who cares?'

During the rehearse stage are you avoiding rehearsing? Are you confident with the transitions in your presentation? Are you pronouncing the content correctly? Rehearsing is a conscious choice: you do it or you don't. Becoming aware will provide you with the option to continue or to change your behavior. If you don't rehearse, ask yourself if you are fine that your delivery becomes your rehearsal.

During the delivery stage handling the saboteur requires a different approach. The most frequently experienced sabotaging is interpreting the audience's behavior.

When we interpret the audience's behavior, presenting gets quickly challenging, because we do not discriminate between fact and fiction. Some speakers interpret the audience's distractions in a negative way and take it personal. It must be about them. It cannot be that a person in the audience might have a valid reason to be distracted. In reality people get distracted all the time. People's minds wander. It's natural. Be honest: how many times do your own thoughts drift when listening to someone else?

The real question is 'are you interpreting the signs correctly?' When your personal motivation sabotages you, you will interpret every sign in a negative way and your presentation will suffer instantly. You might draw a blank, drop your voice, skip slides, say rubbish or mumble. You are no longer connected with your presentation but totally in other people's minds.

Stop interpreting signs and focus on your content immediately. That's the way out of this sabotaging activity pulling you right back where you should be.

GET CLEAR: THE REFERENCE GUIDE

This guide contains two parts. The questions related to Stages 1 & 2, Focus and Prepare. And tips and tricks for Stages 3 & 4 Rehearse and deliver. This is a good moment to take pen and paper and get clear for your next presentation.

▶ Stage 1 Focus

These questions help you become aware of your personal motivation.

1. *What benefits do you expect from presenting?*

2. *What would be the best circumstances for an ideal presenting experience?*

3. *Which circumstances would make it the worst presenting experience?*

4. *Find the underlying beliefs to the best-case and worst-case experiences.*

Find an expectation and ask this question: 'if named expectation were to take place then what would happen?

> Example:
>
> When people connect with me after the presentation I will gain visibility by being an expert. Gaining visibility as an expert will steer my career.

> Example:
>
> If I don't know the answer to a question I might disappoint my line-manager. If I disappoint my line manager I might jeopardize my next promotion.

Continue finding the connections until there is no further answer then you have arrived at the underlying core beliefs. These underlying core beliefs are what drive the personal motivation to act either as an ally or saboteur.

Remember that this process helped Jennifer find her own core beliefs. By discovering them and writing them out we were able to positively influence every stage.

▶ Stage 2 Prepare

Gather information for the event and the audience, craft your content and create a plan B.

Part 1: Event details

Answer the questions below as accurately as you can. 'I do not know', 'I think so', 'I assume', 'probably' and other variations are unclear and can bring about unpleasant surprises. Push back when people tell you, 'it will be fine.' Get clear.

1) *What type of event/presentation is it?*
   Team meeting, an off-site meeting, presentation for auditors are some examples.

2) *What do you know about the room set-up?*
   size, seating arrangements, stage, lectern, etc.

3) *Have you performed a software compatibility check on your final documents?*

4) *Are you being recorded? Is it a live broadcast? How long is your speaking slot and is there a question and answer session?*

5) *Which microphone type are you using, if any. Will there be a sound-check?*
   Tip: Use a headset is my advice.

6) *Who will introduce you and how?*
   Tip: preferably write your own text.

7) *What is the dress code and is there protocol to observe?*

8) *Who is your audience and what is their level of expertise? How much jargon you can use?*

Part 2: Information about the content

1) *What is your presentation's objective?*
   Get clear on your topic. Check the expectations of your audience or check your introduction text.

2) *What information is relevant, which slides need to be included, which details to keep?*
   Keep only what is necessary. When reviewing the content, ask: who cares? Is this information relevant to my audience; if yes, keep, if no, remove.

3) *What information could cause confusion? Find out what is fact based or needs confirmation.*
Only provide information that is clear and confirmed. Avoid over-sharing information for the sake of transparency. Incomplete information causes more harm then good.

Organize your content:

1) *Prepare a catchy opening line that sets the tone but does not reveal the content.*

2) *Have a few key messages adapted to your audience.*

3) *Create a summary: this can be the conclusion of the messages above or a short overview to help the audience gather their thoughts remember your presentation.*

4) *Prepare a catchy closing line. What is it that you want your audience to remember about your presentation?*

Part 4: Plan B

Prevention is better than cure. Most of the stressful experiences during presentations can be avoided with careful preparation and having a plan B ready. Some unpleasant surprises can be prevented while others can easily be dealt with. There are simply no excuses not to have a plan B. And yet, very few presenters spend time on this.

What should you plan for?

Prepare for the question and answer session:

What questions can arise from your content? What questions would stress you when asked? Then find the answers to these questions before presenting. Start with the questions that make you nervous.

Prepare for what might go wrong during your presentation.

Consult your best and worst-case scenarios for the elements you can influence and be creative finding ways to handle the situation now.

For example:
Have your presentation on a USB stick, on your desktop, as an email, in the Cloud

Have copies of the presentation as handouts

Prepare for a presentation of half the allotted time

Bring reserve clothing

Have a substitute in case you fall ill and provide
clear notes

When your presentation is mandatory, find someone who could substitute in case of an emergency. Help your substitute for success by making easy to follow presentation notes. Be as explicit as possible.

Stage 1 and 2 gather all the information you need to create focused and clear content and set you up for success having a plan B. Now it is time to rehearse.

▶ Stage 3 & 4 Rehearse and Deliver Tips

Everybody rehearses; most of us rehearse when we deliver.

You do need to rehearse: But HOW? Here are some tips to get the best from your rehearsals. Jennifer took rehearsals seriously resulting in an impactful delivery.

1. **Rehearse OUT LOUD**

   As a presenter you need to hear yourself deliver the message and find out which parts you struggle with. Keep practicing until you are confident with the content.

Presenting in a language other than your mother tongue is stressful. Learn to pronounce the words correctly. If you're a native speaker, adapt the speed of your delivery so people can understand you. Rehearsing will tell you how quickly you speak.

2. **Rehearse in the same position which you will present**

Rehearsing in the position from which you will present will help you access appropriate body language and vocal variety.

When you rehearse on stage:

Rehearse walking on and off stage. Become familiar with the speaking area, lectern and technology used.

3. **Rehearse until you know your presentation inside out**

There might come a moment when you think: 'I know it well enough'. Still, rehearse one last time.

4. **Use a mirror to get the final criticism:**

Your own inner critic gives the most honest feedback. When you can handle that, you will remain confident. Rehearse at least once in front of the mirror.

5. **Ask for feedback: Have a least 1 person watch your presentation prior to delivery**

Rehearsal is the ideal time to get feedback. Better to have the feedback now than after your presentation.

6. **Play the game of extremes to crack the mold of seriousness.**

An excellent way to release the seriousness and release blocking stress is to give the presentation using two extreme techniques. They force you to use a delivery style that is totally inappropriate to the content and this helps you find your speaking voice in sync with the message. Do this exercise with a few lines of your presentation following the three steps.

Step 1: rehearse the presentation as if it is the funniest information you have ever shared. Go for it and find your humor.

Step 2: rehearse the same presentation as if it is the most serious information you have ever shared.

Step 3: Shake off, loosen up and start again. You have just cracked the mold of being too serious.

7. **Warm up your voice before speaking**

Using tongue twisters to warm up your voice and make your facial muscles flexible. By using them it will make you feel more confident during your presentation. Using tongue twisters provides fun and lightens the moods. Some fun examples in English:

A twister of twists once twisted a twist;
A twist that he twisted was a three-twisted twist;
If in twisting a twist one twist should untwist,
The untwisted twist would untwist the twist.

Silly Sally swiftly shooed seven silly sheep.
The seven silly sheep Silly Sally shooed
swiftly sailed south.

Sandra Van de Cauter

**These sheep shouldn't sleep in a shack;
sheep should sleep in a shed.**

LET'S BUST SOME MYTHS

I'd like to highlight myths I heard during my years of coaching and bust them once and for all. These myths are damaging to the credibility of every presenter.

Myth 1: Focus on the Alpha Dog

The first time I heard the term Alpha dog was about 6 years ago. Honestly I wasn't sure what they were talking about. Finally, I understood they meant the decision maker in the meeting. The advice given was to look for the Alpha Dog and present towards him or her. No kidding. My advice, if you see a dog in the meeting room, call security.

There is no such thing as an Alpha Dog during meetings and presentations. There might be senior and more senior people present, but definitely no dogs.

Accept that everyone in the meeting room is or should be there for a reason. Focus on your audience. Besides, you might be mistaken about who the decision maker is. What if you focus the whole time on one person and the real decision maker is someone you ignored?

Myth 2: It's Better To Give Any Answer Than No Answer At All

A line-manage once advised a colleague to always answer a question.

'If you do not know the answer, invent one!'

That is a fast way to lose your credibility. When you do not know the answer, do not invent one for the sake of answering. Be honest.

Myth 3: Prolonging My Presentation To Avoid The Question And Answer Session

So many people in the business dread the question and answer session. Their inner soundtrack says *'What if I do not know the answer? What questions might surprise me? I hope they do not ask too many questions.'*

A question and answer session is an opportunity to provide clarity. That's all.

Running over time to preclude a question and answer session is more an indication you are insufficiently prepared.

Myth 4: I Have To Answer All The Questions, Even Those Unrelated To The Presentation

No. It is totally acceptable to ask your colleagues to relate their questions to the presentation.

Myth 5: I Should Be Able To Present Like ___ (You Fill In The Name)

No, you shouldn't. Think of Oscar Wilde's quote: *'Be yourself; everyone else is already taken.'* People like to see you present and be yourself.

CLOSING WORDS

I believe presenting is serious. Presenters put their credibility on the line. Do you want to leave an impact? Do you want to keep or build your credibility? Do you want to make a difference? An impactful presentation worth hearing can help you do this.

This book captures elements for giving impactful presentations. Even if you only have a couple of hours to prepare a presentation, you will be far more successful by going through the different stages and get clear on your content rather than jumping behind your computer and throwing slides together. I have applied this approach with dozens of leaders and even only one hour working together made a huge impact. Once you get clear everything else unfolds.

Jennifer inspired me to look at coaching differently. The personal motivation became the reason why speakers are successful or not. Everyone can make a difference every time they present. It only takes one person to make that difference. You!

Get Clear. Craft and Deliver Impactful Business Presentations Worth Hearing. Start Today.

ACKNOWLEDGEMENTS

Writing a book on a topic I am passionate about has been more challenging then I had thought. Over and over again I found myself procrastinating, finding all kinds of excuses. In other moments I wanted to rush, get it finished, get it out. I had a hard time getting clear.

Until the day I realized I was experiencing the sabotaging effects of the same effect I was writing about: the personal motivation. In other words, I experienced first-hand how powerfully accurate the teachings of this book are. I was writing from experience.

Luckily I have encountered many people I talked to about the book and who were eager to see me finish it. It gave me a boost. It provided me with enough courage to continue.

I thank the many people I had the pleasure to work with over the last years and whom have experienced the developing of the stages described in this book. I value the trust that they have shown in accepting and applying 'Get Clear'.

I thank C. Piccolo for her everlasting support, gently making me aware of my own sabotaging actions and effortlessly editing the content. A special 'thank you' to M. Platt who led me through the birth of a book and pushed me to think differently. I also express my deepest gratitude to the board of BPW Basel Anglo for inspiring me.

Writing this book has been a personal journey that made me believe strongly in the power of 'Get Clear'.

Sandra

www.sandravandecauter.ch